Content

New
Boots

Written by Lianna Rogers
Illustrated by Jennifer Cooper

We put on our new boots.

2

We jump in a puddle.
Our boots go
splash!

We walk in the grass.
Our boots go
swish!

3

We slide in the mud.
Our boots go
splosh!

We run into the house.
Our boots go...

Fun Island

You are on Fun Island.

Find your way to the campsite.

What can you do on Fun Island?

F G H I

N
W E
S

Danger!

Fun Island Campsite

Welcome

7

Water

one Fishing!

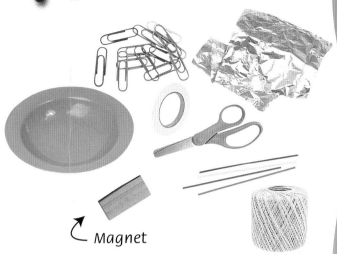

Magnet

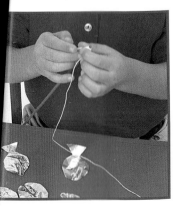

W
w
W
w
W
w
W
w
W

waterfall

wo

Go

Find
that
the

1

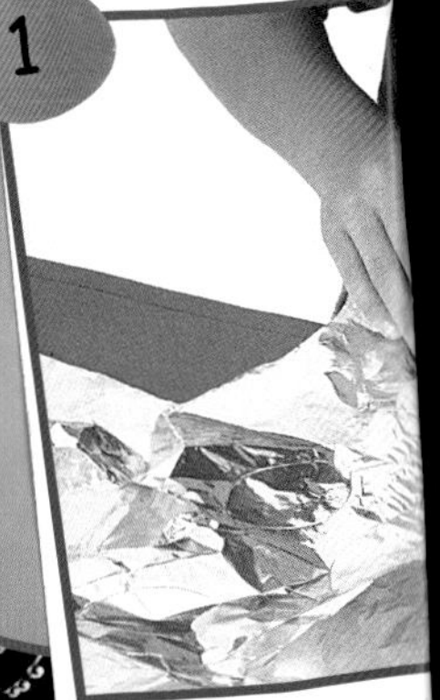

2

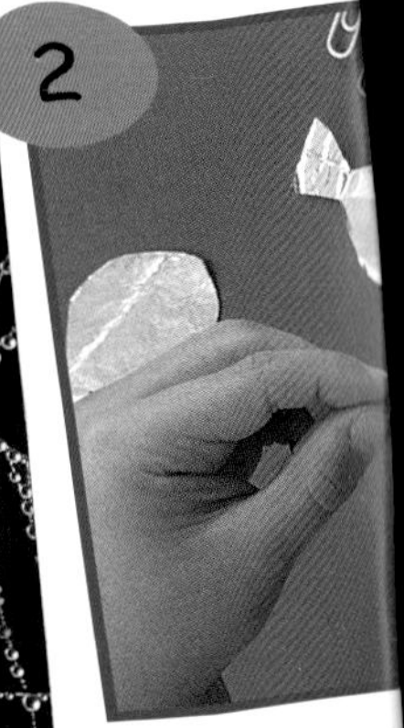

3

wand

wet

water

wheel

wave

Find the words that begin with the letter w.

waterfall

web

8

Gone Fishing!

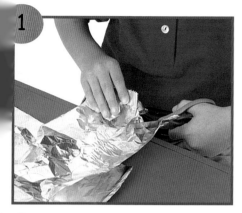

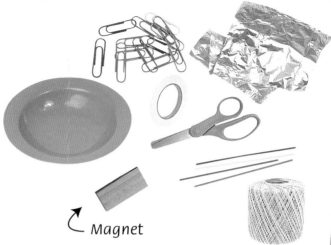

$\curvearrowleft$ Magnet

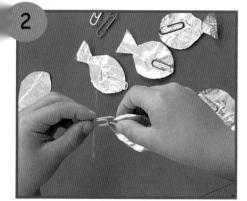

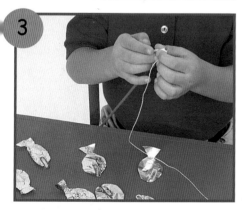

Play

What can you do with water?

On Monday It Rained

Written by Marie Gibson   Illustrated by Ian Forss

14

15

On Monday it rained.
Horse got wet.
He did not like it.

16

On Tuesday it rained.
Sheep got wet.
She did not like it.

17

On Wednesday it rained.
Goat got wet.
He did not like it.

18

On Thursday it rained.
Cow got wet.
She did not like it.

On Friday it rained.
Dog got wet.
He did not like it.

20

On Saturday it rained.
Cat got wet.
She did not like it.

21

On Sunday it rained.
I got wet.

I liked it!

Rain

Rain on the roses.

Rain on the bus.

Rain on the river.

But don't rain on us!

24

25

Splish, Splosh, Splash!

Written by Josh Ryan

Penguins can swim.
They swim in the water.

Penguins can leap.
They leap out of the water.

Penguins can walk.
They walk on the ground.

Penguins can slide.
They slide on the ice.

Can penguins fly?
No! But...

...penguins can jump!
They jump into the water.

Splish, splosh, splash!

33

Wet Pet

A pet! A pet!

A net! A net!

A pet in a net!

Wet,
wet,
wet!

Letters I Know

 Bb **Rr**  **Ww**

Sounds I Know

 **-et**

Words I Know

can	he	not	they
did	in	on	we
go	it	our	
got	like	she	

36